The Night Before Christmas in the Manger

Written by
Sara Broyhill Anderson

Illustrated by
Julia Moroko

BNA Publishing LLC

Austin, TX

THE NIGHT BEFORE CHRISTMAS IN THE MANGER
Text and Illustrations @2024 Sara Broyhill Anderson.
admin@sarabroyhillanderson.com
Illustrations by Julia Moroko.

All rights reserved. No portion of this book may be reproduced in any form without the written permission of the publisher, with the exception of brief excerpts in reviews.

BNA Publishing LLC
PO Box 90453
Austin, TX 78709
USA

ISBN: 978-1-7362329-6-5 (hardback non-jacket)

ISBN: 978-1-7362329-7-2 (paperback)

It was the night before Christmas, and all 'round the tree, sat my mom, and my dad, my sister and me.

"Tonight," said my mom, "let's read the great story, the birth of our Savior, God's plan of great glory."

Joseph in his robe and Mary with her belly,
had started a journey, both watchful and wary.

They went to be counted per the Roman decree,
to Bethlehem in Judea from a town in Galilee.

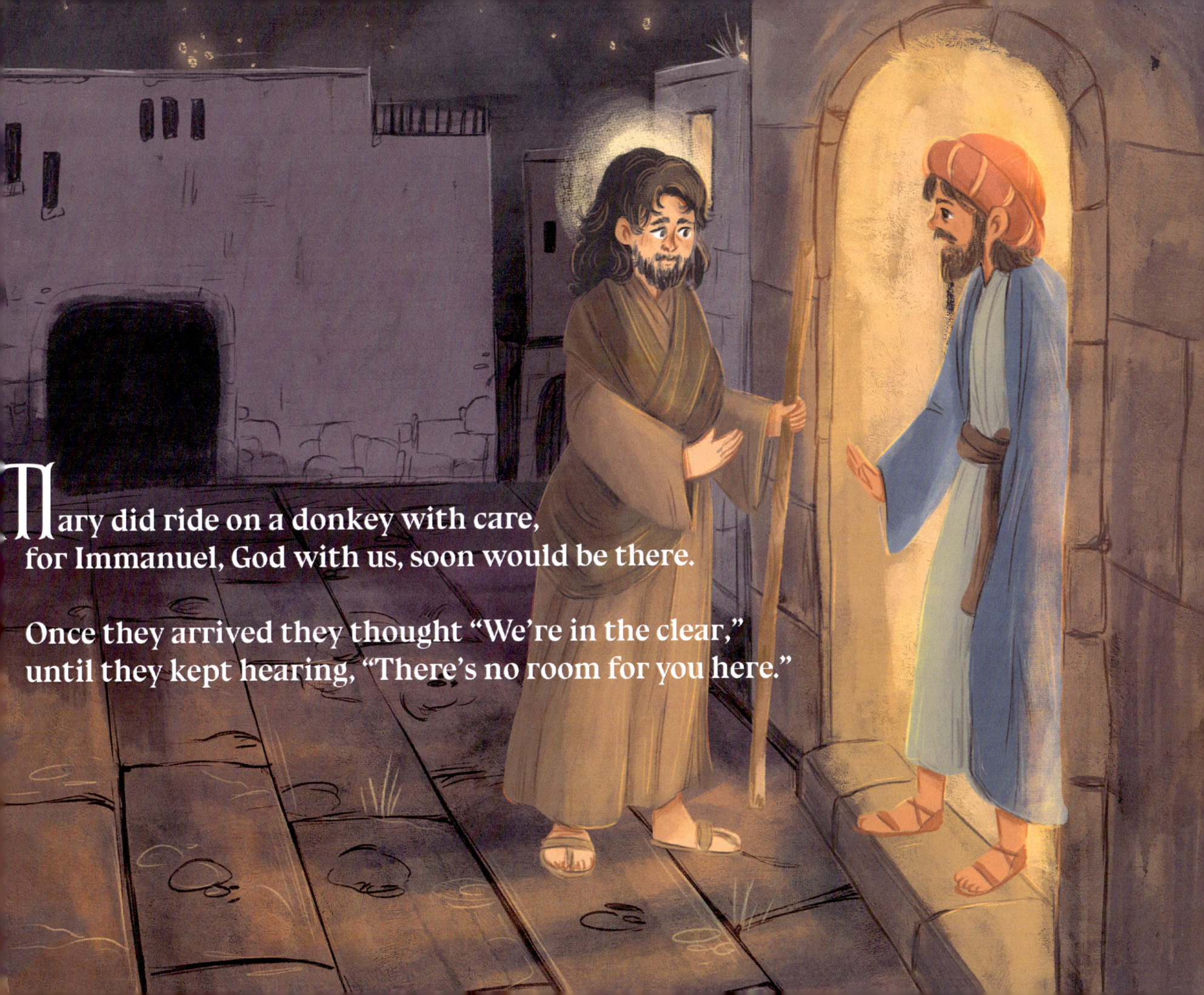

Mary did ride on a donkey with care,
for Immanuel, God with us, soon would be there.

Once they arrived they thought "We're in the clear,"
until they kept hearing, "There's no room for you here."

One single voice stood out from the rest,
"You can sleep in the stable, though it isn't the best."

Now Joseph and Mary were all snuggled in bed,
while visions of God's kingdom danced in their head.

Then what to their wondering eyes should appear?
Christ Jesus! Born next to the goats, sheep, and steer.

Wrapped in a swaddling cloth to keep warm,
He was laid in a manger (which wasn't the norm).

The Shepherds who tended their flocks in the night
got news of Christ's birth from the angels in flight.

The stars in the sky looked down where he lay,
and led the stunned shepherds to the babe in the hay.

Then came the Wise men from far in the east,
to see for themselves the professed Prince of Peace.

Gifts of gold, frankincense, and even of myrrh,
presented these Magi to salute His great birth.

Now wise men! Now shepherds! Now all of the nations!
On peoples! On places! From every station!

Praise the Lord! Mighty God! The one who transcends!
Born at the right time, His kingdom won't end!

With justice and righteousness forevermore.
No fear—only love, more than we could ask for.

"That's not the end," said my mom, "there's more to the story."
"Christ died for our sins and will return in great glory."

"Christ saved us because we cannot save ourselves,"
It's his free gift of grace—much greater than wealth."

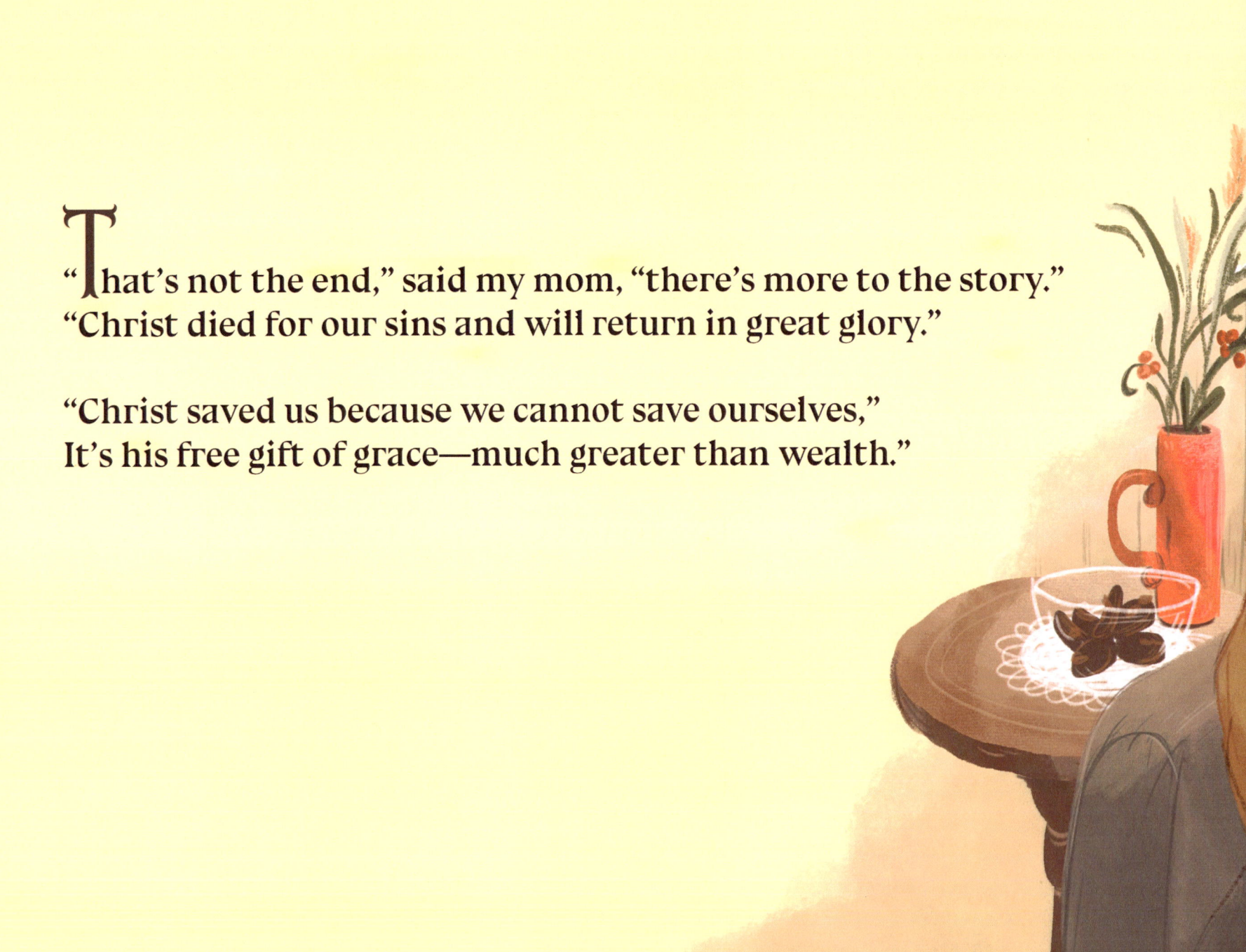

"So we wait and we pray
for His kingdom to come.
God is patient and kind
and loves everyone."

"Wow!" I thought

as my dad tucked me in tight...

"*Merry Christmas*

to all, and to all a

blessed night."

www.ingramcontent.com/pod-product-compliance
Lightning Source LLC
Chambersburg PA
CBRC101521070526
44585CB00010B/177